Dealing With Waste

OLD CARS

Sally Morgan

A⁺

Smart Apple Media

This book has been published in cooperation with Franklin Watts.

Editor: Rachel Minay, Designer: Brenda Cole, Picture research: Morgan Interactive Ltd., Consultant: Graham Williams

Picture credits:
The publishers would like to thank the following for reproducing these photographs: Alamy 24 (Chuck Pefley); Corbis 9 (Alain Denize/Sygma), 18 (Peter Yates); Digitalvision front cover main image; Ecoscene front cover top right (Ian Harwood), 6 (Jon Bower), 7 (Angela Hampton), 8 (Andrew Brown), 10 (Alex Bartel), 11 (Rosemary Greenwood), 12 (Anthony Cooper), 13 (Angela Hampton), 15 (Vicki Coombs), 16 (Tony Page), 17 (Mark Tweedie), 19 (Ceanne Jensen), 20 (Paul Kennedy), 21 (Guy Stubbs), 22 (Vicki Coombs), 23 (Stephen Coyne) 25 (Sally Morgan), 26 (Adrian Morgan), 27 (Mike Maidment); Recyclenow.com front cover bottom right.

Published in the United States by Smart Apple Media
2140 Howard Drive West, North Mankato, Minnesota 56003

Library of Congress Cataloging-in-Publication Data

Morgan, Sally.
Old cars / by Sally Morgan.
p. cm. – (Dealing with waste)
Includes index.
ISBN-13: 978-1-59920-010-1
1. Automobiles–Materials–Recycling. I. Title.

TL154.M588 2007
363.72'88–dc22   2006035138

9 8 7 6 5 4 3 2 1

Contents

Millions of cars

There are hundreds of millions of cars in the world. Each year the number goes up as millions more cars are manufactured.

Cars around the world

The number of cars is rapidly increasing in countries such as China and India. As these countries become more developed, people can afford to buy cars. In countries such as the United States, the United Kingdom (UK), Germany, and Australia, owning a car is very common, and many families have two or even three cars.

Not only do cars pollute the air, they cause traffic jams in cities.

Burning fuel

Cars need fuel, and this fuel comes from oil. Oil is a type of fossil fuel formed underground over millions of years from the remains of plants and animals. However, oil supplies are running out. Oil is unsustainable and is being used up much faster than new oil can be made.

The car engine produces gases when the fuel is burned. These gases include carbon dioxide and nitrogen oxides. They can cause air pollution in such forms as acid rain and smog. Acid rain damages trees and buildings around the world. Carbon dioxide is a greenhouse gas that traps heat in the Earth's atmosphere. It contributes to global warming.

People depend on cars to get around in their daily lives, for example when they are shopping or traveling to work or school. The use of public transportation has declined in recent years.

It's my world!

How many cars does your family own? Can you figure out how many miles your family travels in a car each week? How could you cut down on the number of miles? Could you use public transportation for some trips?

Getting rid of old cars

One of the biggest problems today is disposing of all of the old cars when they come to the end of their lives. Many resources were used to make these cars, so it is important that as much as possible be recycled.

In this book, you will read about the different materials that are used to build cars and how a car can be broken into pieces and recycled at the end of its life.

Car parts

A car is a complex piece of machinery. A typical family car is made of about 15,000 separate parts. These are made from many different raw materials.

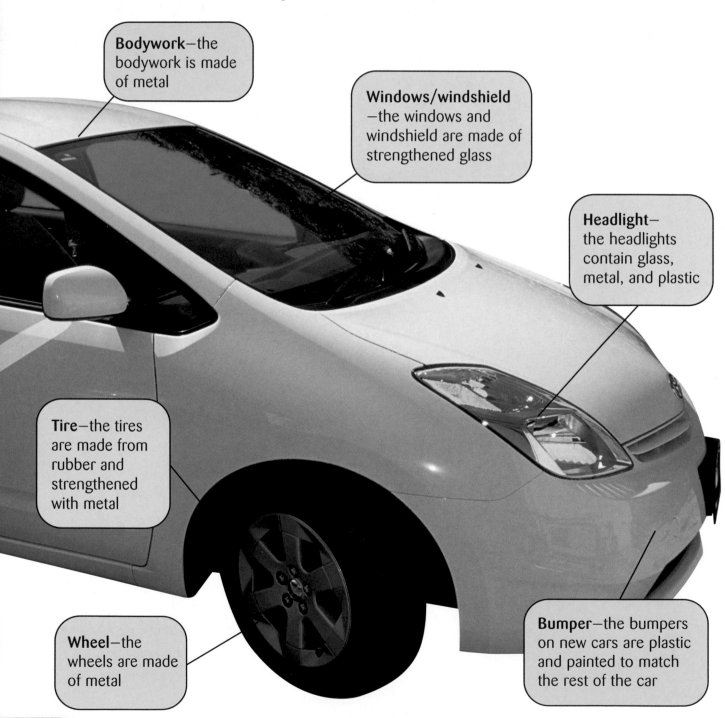

Bodywork—the bodywork is made of metal

Windows/windshield—the windows and windshield are made of strengthened glass

Headlight—the headlights contain glass, metal, and plastic

Tire—the tires are made from rubber and strengthened with metal

Wheel—the wheels are made of metal

Bumper—the bumpers on new cars are plastic and painted to match the rest of the car

Raw materials

Car manufacturing requires iron, steel, aluminum, zinc, lead, copper, platinum, and a range of other materials such as glass and plastic. The body of a car is made of an underbody, or floor pan, sides, and a roof. It must be strong enough to protect the people inside, so it is made from a metal such as steel. The metal is covered in many layers of paint and a top layer of wax to protect the paint. The inside of the bodywork is covered with plastics and fabric. The seats are made from foam and covered with fabric or leather.

A number of materials are used inside a car. This car's dashboard is made of plastic with dials of glass and metal, while the seats and steering wheel are covered in leather.

Engine and exhaust

A car's engine and exhaust pipe are made from a metal such as steel or aluminum. When the fuel burns inside the engine, it produces hot gases that expand rapidly and push on the piston. This causes the wheels to turn. The gases leave the engine via the exhaust. There is also a fuel tank and pipes to supply the engine with fuel. The engine is connected to a gearbox, clutch, and braking system. Extensive wiring controls the engine, lights, and alarm system. The wiring is covered in a protective plastic sleeve.

In addition, there are windows made from glass and lots of pieces of plastic such as the bumpers, wheel arches, and door handles.

A car's life

Cars are made in factories. A modern factory has a long assembly line where the frame of the car is moved on a conveyor belt past robots and workers who add parts to the car.

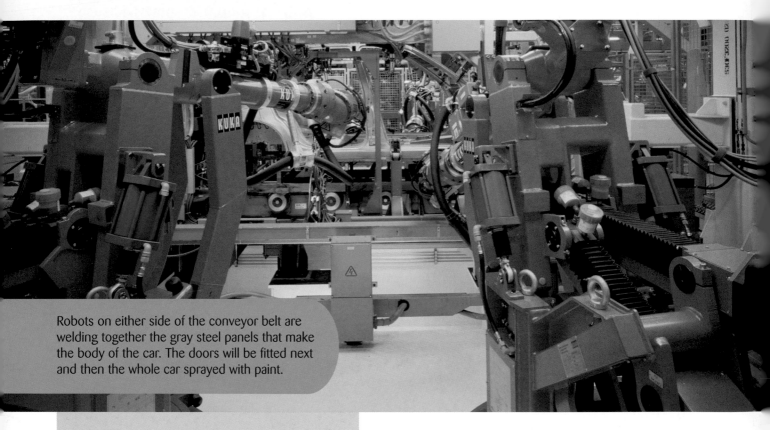

Robots on either side of the conveyor belt are welding together the gray steel panels that make the body of the car. The doors will be fitted next and then the whole car sprayed with paint.

Did you know . . .

It is estimated that about 30 tons (27 t) of waste are produced during the extraction of the raw materials that are needed to make one car.

Preparing the bodywork

In the press shop, a huge sheet of metal is cut into shapes that make the car body. Robots build the floor pan of the car, leaving spaces for the wheel arches and boot wells. Then the sides and roof are welded into place. Doors are made and attached to the body. Once the bodywork is complete, lasers check the surface for the smallest fault. The car is cleaned, rinsed, and moved to the paint shop where paint is sprayed over the body with a finishing layer of wax.

Making the inside

The next stage is to make the inside of the car. First the wiring is put in place, then the carpets are laid, followed by the seats and other fittings. The windshield and windows are glued into place. Finally, the engine, clutch, and transmission are lowered into position. The fuel tank is positioned toward the back of the car. Once the engine is in place, the suspension, steering, radiator, and battery are added, and then the wheels and tires. Finally, water, antifreeze, oil, and fuel are added so that the car engine can be turned on and tested. Now it is ready to be transported to the dealers who sell the cars.

It's my world!

Look closely at your family's car. How many different materials have been used on the exterior bodywork? How many other materials have been used to make the seats and to line the interior of the car?

Too many vehicles are abandoned at the end of their lives rather than being disposed of properly.

Repair or scrap?

A modern car has a lifespan of about 10–15 years. It can be repaired when something goes wrong, and parts of the body can be replaced if they are damaged in accidents. However, cars are expensive to repair, so an older car is often scrapped if it has been in a serious accident or if the engine needs replacing. Many countries have strict rules controlling the disposal of cars. Often, the owner must pay to have a car scrapped.

Reduce, reuse, and recycle

More cars mean that more of the world's resources are being used in manufacturing. More cars also mean that more fuel is burned and there is more congestion on the roads. Somehow, the number of cars on the roads must be reduced. This can be achieved by reducing, reusing, and recycling.

Reducing the number of cars

One way to solve the problem of disposing of old cars is to make fewer cars in the first place. A good public transport system means people can get around without having to buy a car. People could use trains or buses rather than cars. Many cars on the road are occupied by just one person. If more people shared cars, there would be fewer cars on the road.

School buses such as this one transport large numbers of students to and from school, so fewer individual trips are made by car.

Reusing cars

An older car can cost a lot of money to repair, so old cars are often scrapped rather than repaired. Cheaper repairs would help make the car last longer. Car designers could help. They could design the car so that the engine and other parts are easy to access for repair. The bodywork should be easy to remove and replace. Much of a car repair bill is not the cost of spare parts but the cost of the labor to carry out the repair. Often, the engine must be removed to replace a part, which takes a lot of time. If more thought was put into car engine design, these costs could be reduced.

It's my world!

Think before you get in a car. Is the journey necessary? Could you walk or cycle instead? Could you take a bus or train? If more people used public transportation, there would be fewer cars on the roads and less congestion in towns and cities. Walking and cycling are the most environmentally friendly options because no fuel is needed.

Recycling cars

Eventually a car reaches the end of its life and must be scrapped. It is important that as much of the car as possible is recycled.

These cars are called end-of-life vehicles. In the United States, as many as 10 million vehicles are scrapped each year. A modern car is designed so that it can be taken apart and recycled more easily than in the past. In the European Union, there are laws that make the car manufacturer responsible for the disposal of end-of-life vehicles.

This family is using bicycles to get around town rather than driving in a car.

Metal recycling

The bodywork of a car is usually made of metal, along with the engine and other parts such as the exhaust. Metals are valuable materials and can be recycled over and over again without any loss of quality.

Steel and aluminum

Cars contain a lot of steel and aluminum in the bodywork and the engine. The bodywork is made of thin metal so that it is strong but does not weigh too much. Aluminum is used in cars because it is a lighter metal than steel. A car engine made from aluminum rather than steel weighs much less, so the car uses less fuel. The main part of the engine is often made from recycled aluminum foil. Scrap aluminum is heated until it melts. The molten metal is poured into molds to make ingots (large blocks of pure metal) then sold to car manufacturers.

Molten aluminum is a red hot liquid. Here it is being poured into molds.

Extracting metal

It is cheaper and more efficient to recycle metals because only a few metals, such as gold, can be taken straight from the ground. Most metals occur in the form of a metal ore. The ores are dug from the ground in mines or quarries. This creates a lot of waste in the form of soil and rock. Habitats are lost, and the mining operation causes harmful pollution.

The ore is crushed and then transported to the refinery. This is often on the other side of the world. Finally, the ore is processed so that the metal comes out and can be used. This uses lots of energy and creates even more pollution.

The metal from scrapped cars is shredded and then sent to a factory for melting down.

Did you know . . .

Modern cars contain a catalytic converter within the exhaust system. It absorbs harmful gases so that the car produces less air pollution. The catalytic converter is a stainless steel tube containing metals such as platinum, rhodium, or palladium. These are valuable metals, so it is well worth recycling the converters.

Melting and recycling

Metals are easy to recycle. First, they are sorted into types. Steel can be separated from aluminum by using a magnet. Then, they are simply heated until they melt. They can be rolled or shaped into a new object. Although energy is needed to melt the metal, this is far less than the energy required to extract and transport the ore. Metals can be recycled over and over again without losing any of their properties.

Plastics

Throughout the last 30 years, the plastic content of an average vehicle has more than tripled, from about 70.5 pounds (32 kg) in 1970 to 251 pounds (114 kg) today. That's about 11 percent of a car. Plastic parts include the bumpers, the car interior, and mats.

Lightweight plastics

Plastics are lighter than many alternative materials. For example, a part made from plastic weighs half as much as the same part made in steel. This means that a car with a high plastic content is much lighter in weight but just as strong. A lighter car does not use as much fuel. For example, a reduction in car weight of 660 pounds (300 kg) saves about 264 gallons (1,000 l) of fuel during the average life of a car.

Long-lasting plastics

Plastics have other valuable properties. They do not rust like steel—so they can be used on the outside of the car—and they do not need to be covered by a protective layer of paint. Plastic parts last a long time, and they do not scratch or dent as easily as metal. They are also cheaper to make. Plastics can be made into shapes that would be impossible with metals and have allowed car designers to produce exciting car designs.

Did you know ...

Most modern cars have bumpers painted the same color as the body. This causes problems during recycling because the paint must be removed before the plastic can be recycled and this is increasing the cost. Manufacturers are looking for ways to remove the paint cheaply.

Car designers must make sure that the plastic parts of a car can be easily removed and recycled.

This pile of plastic waste is waiting to be recycled. Plastics are sorted, cleaned, and then broken into small flakes that can be poured into large sacks and taken to factories to make plastics.

Recycling plastic

The higher plastic content of a modern car means it is important to reuse or recycle as much as possible at the end of a car's life. The various parts are removed, sorted into types of plastic, and either sold as secondhand replacement parts or sent to plastic recycling companies to be processed. One problem with removing and sorting all the plastics is the cost. Often, it can cost more to remove, identify, and process the plastic than it would to buy new.

Car manufacturers are also using more recycled plastic to make new plastic parts. Soft drink bottles are being recycled into engine parts, while old carpeting made of nylon (a synthetic fabric made from oil) is being recycled into parts for the fan in the engine. Ford, one of the world's largest car manufacturers, wants its suppliers to make plastic car parts with at least 25 percent recycled plastic content.

Problem tires

A tire is made mostly from rubber, steel, and textiles such as cotton. Tires must be replaced when they wear down or get punctured. When a tire comes to the end of its life, it can be reused, recycled, buried in a landfill, or burned.

Old tires have just been dumped on this beach. This is a waste of resources because the materials in a tire are valuable and could be reused or recycled.

Burning tires

Tires can be burned, but they produce a lot of black smoke. If tires have to be burned, the best place is in an incinerator, where the pollution can be controlled and the heat used to generate electricity. Some cement manufacturers burn tires instead of coal as a source of heat in the kilns where cement is made. This reduces the amount of coal that is used.

Did you know ...

In the U.S., about 290 million tires were scrapped in 2003 alone. About 80 percent of these tires were reused or recycled, but the rest ended up in landfills or were dumped in the countryside. In the UK, about 50 million tires are scrapped each year, most of which are reused or recycled.

Reusing tires

Tires can be used in new and creative ways. For example, they can be used as plant containers in the garden or swings in a playground. They are even used to build new coral reefs along some tropical coasts. Tires in good condition can be made into retreads.

The old tread is removed and a new tread stuck in its place. Retreading allows the tire to be used longer and avoids having to buy a new tire. Retreads are cheap to buy, but they are not as safe as new tires. Cars fitted with retreads cannot be driven at high speeds.

These men in South Africa are cutting up old tires and painting them to use as decorative features in a garden.

Recycling tires

The rubber from a tire can be cut up to make mats and shoe soles. It can be shredded into crumbs and used to make flooring, playground and road surfaces, carpet underlay, and noise insulation, as well as new tires. Now that there are so many uses for old tires, they have become more valuable and fewer are thrown away.

It's my world!

Look for things that have been made with old tires. For example, an old tire can be used to make a plant container or the seat of a swing. See if the surface of your local playground is made from rubber. Some boots are also made from recycled rubber.

Batteries

Cars need a battery to start the engine. A typical car battery is a 12 V lead-acid battery, which consists of a plastic container containing several pieces of lead surrounded by an acid solution. There are two metal knobs on the top that are connected to wires from the engine.

Starting the engine

A battery stores electricity. When the key is turned in the ignition, the battery delivers a short burst of power to the starter motor, which starts the engine. Each time this happens, the battery loses some of its stored electricity, but it is recharged when the car engine is running. Eventually the battery goes flat and it must be replaced.

Recycling batteries

Most car batteries are recycled. Old batteries are swapped for new ones at garages, and the garages send the old ones for recycling. During the recycling process, the acid is drained away and the battery is hammered into pieces. To separate the different materials, the pieces are dropped into a large container of liquid, where the plastic pieces float and the heavy lead parts sink. Often, the lead and plastic in a lead-acid battery have been recycled many times. A typical lead-acid battery contains 60–80 percent recycled lead and plastic.

These batteries have been taken from scrapped cars. If they are not sold, they will be sent for recycling.

Did you know . . .

Recycling lead-acid batteries is a success story in the U.S. Each year, nearly 99 million lead-acid car batteries are made, and 97 percent of them are recycled.

Dry batteries

The lead-acid battery in a car is very different from the small alkaline batteries used in electrical goods such as toys and personal stereos. However, alkaline batteries also contain metals that can be recycled. Some alkaline batteries can be recharged and used again, but most must be thrown away when they are flat. These should be taken to battery recycling centers where they can be collected and the parts recycled.

Somebody has dumped a pile of car batteries and tires in the countryside. The contents of the car batteries could pollute the ground and harm wildlife.

Glass recycling

Cars contain glass in the windows and the lights. The glass used in cars is different from that used in bottles because it needs to be strengthened for safety.

Windshields

In the past, a shattered windshield was a common sight. Now windshields are made from laminated glass. This is glass that is made of two layers stuck together with a plastic glue. Laminated glass is used because it does not shatter when damaged but stays as one complete piece of glass. Windshields often need to be repaired because the glass has been chipped by gravel and other bits flying up from the road surface.

Windshields often have heating elements attached to the glass to melt any ice, which make recycling them more difficult.

A small chip in a windshield can usually be repaired, but large cracks are dangerous, and the whole windshield should be replaced.

Toughened glass

The other windows in a car are made from toughened glass, which does not break as easily as a pane of glass. Sometimes these windows are tinted. Tinting is achieved by painting the glass or adding resins to it during manufacturing. Tinted glass is more difficult to recycle because of the color.

Modern cars have large glass windows that give the driver good visibility. Most of the glass can be recycled, but tinted glass is more difficult. Unfortunately, cars with tinted windows are becoming more common.

Removing glass

The glass in a car is stuck in place and can be difficult to remove. Most scrap yards have to break it with a hammer, which is dangerous and often leaves bits of glass attached to the bodywork. The broken glass is collected by a glass recycling company. Car glass is crushed and used to make things such as glass tiles. The plastic glue in laminated glass is very expensive to buy, so it is recycled.

Often, just the plastic from between the layers of glass in the windshield is recycled, while the glass is sent to a landfill.

Only a small percentage of glass from a car is recycled at present because of the problems of removal. Car manufacturers need to deal with these problems if more glass from cars is to be recycled in the future.

The way ahead

One way to reduce the number of cars being manufactured is to reduce the need for cars. Fewer cars on the road means that fewer cars will end up in scrap yards.

Fewer cars in cities

There are many groups around the world that try to persuade people to leave their cars behind and use public transportation. Many of the major roads leading into cities have High Occupancy Vehicle (HOV) lanes for cars with three or more people. This encourages carpooling. In London and Singapore, vehicles entering the center of the city are charged an entry fee. In London this is called congestion charging. This is to discourage people from bringing their cars into the city.

School buses help to reduce congestion, too. A bus may carry 40 or 50 students, which lessens the need for lots of individual cars to be driven to a school.

The center of Singapore is a restricted zone; cars must pay money to enter it. This discourages people from driving their cars in the city.

Fewer resources

Large cars use more raw materials in their manufacture. So if more people bought small cars, the demand for raw materials would decrease. Smaller cars weigh less and do not require as much fuel. When a car must be scrapped, it is important that as much as possible is recycled. Currently, between 75 and 80 percent of the materials (by weight) in an end-of-life vehicle are recycled in countries in the European Union and North America. This figure could be higher still.

The Smart car is one of a new range of small cars. It is just 8.2 feet (2.5 m) long and uses only 0.92 gallons (3.5 l) of fuel to travel 62 miles (100 km).

It's my world!

In the UK, half of all car trips are less than 3 miles (5 km). These trips could be made on foot or by bicycle. Short car rides are the most damaging to the environment. Catalytic converters are only effective for journeys over 3 miles (5 km,) and the first half mile (1 km) produces 60 percent more fumes. Try to avoid using a car for short trips, and use a bike or walk instead.

Long lifespan

In the past, the life of a car was around 20 or 30 years. This was because cars were very expensive to buy and people did not replace them often. Now, a car's lifespan is 10 to 15 years. People can afford to replace cars more frequently because the cost of a new car has decreased compared with earnings, and often the cost of repairing an old car is more than the car is worth.

Glossary

Assembly line
a factory system where each worker carries out a particular job as the object (such as a car) passes by on a moving track

Battery
a device that stores electricity

Congestion
the build-up of traffic on streets

Coolant
a fluid that is used to carry heat away from something

Developed country
a country in which most people have a high standard of living

Exhaust
a system through which hot gases are allowed to escape

Fossil fuel
a fuel formed over millions of years from the remains of plants and animals, for example, peat, coal, crude oil, and natural gas

Global warming
the gradual warming of the average temperature of Earth, caused by an increase in greenhouse gases

Greenhouse gas
a gas in the atmosphere that traps heat

Landfill
a large hole in the ground that is used to dispose of waste

Ore
a type of rock that contains metal in sufficient quantity to be mined

Ozone layer
a layer high in Earth's atmosphere that absorbs harmful ultraviolet rays from the sun

Pollution
the release of harmful substances into the environment

Recycle
to process and reuse materials in order to make new items

Reduce
to lower the amount of waste that is produced

Reuse
to use something again, either in the same way or in a different way

Scrap yard
a place where end-of-life vehicles are taken to be broken up

Smog
dust, smoke, and chemical fumes that pollute the air and make it hazy

Unsustainable
a level of use of a resource that cannot be maintained into the future and which will cause the resource to run out

Welding
joining metals together using heat

Web sites

Cars and the Environment
www.savethekoala.com/
koalastips.html
Australian Web page giving lots of advice about how you can recycle and cut down on waste.

Car Recycling
www.wastepoint.co.uk/media/
factsheets/Cars.pdf
Web page covering end-of-life vehicles and how they can be recycled.

Earth 911
www.earth911.org/master.asp
This Web site shows a variety of national and local U.S. recycling programs and events.

Plastics and Cars
www.plastics-car.com/s_plasticscar/
doc.asp?CID=407&DID=1608
Web page giving information about the use of plastics in cars and how they are recycled.

Recycle Now: Tire Recycling
www.recyclenow.com/at_leisure/
tyre_recycling.html
Part of a useful Web site on all aspects of recycling, this Web page discusses the life of a recycled tire.

Recycling Tires
www.ohiodnr.com/recycling/awareness/
facts/tires
This Web site provides an introduction to tire and rubber recycling.

U.S. Environmental Protection Agency
www.epa.gov
This Web site has lots of environmental information on all issues, not just waste. There is an EPA Kids Club (www.epa.gov/kids) with information on waste and recycling.

U.S. Environmental Protection Agency: Batteries
www.epa.gov/epaoswer/non-hw/
muncpl/battery.htm
This page gives information about batteries.

Index